I0210944

Resettlement

poems by

Clinton Smith

Finishing Line Press
Georgetown, Kentucky

Resettlement

Copyright © 2024 by Clinton Smith
ISBN 979-8-88838-463-3 First Edition
All rights reserved under International and Pan-American Copyright Conventions.
No part of this book may be reproduced in any manner whatsoever without written
permission from the publisher, except in the case of brief quotations embodied in
critical articles and reviews.

ACKNOWLEDGMENTS

I'd like to thank everyone who was instrumental in helping "Resettlement"
in specific, and my poetry practice in general, evolve to the (still quite
imperfect) place it is today: Leonard Gontarek, whose poetry workshop
helped hone many specific craft elements in my work, and refine my reading
of poetry; Kelly Lambiras and Lake Angela, for being advocates of my work;
Lisa Sewell and Peter Balakian for commenting on early drafts of the work
and providing me with some directions I could follow when revising; and
my writers' group in Philadelphia (Matthew Barbehenn, Jeremy Hauck,
Sonja Crafts, and Elizabeth Spencer) for continuing to provide input that (I
hope) improves the work as it continues.

And, finally, I thank my family, the aforementioned Elizabeth and my
2 children, Hannah and Colin, for being an inspiration, and tolerating
someone who hops up at all hours of the day and night to write, walking
around the house in thought rather loudly in the process.

Publisher: Leah Huete de Maines
Editor: Christen Kincaid
Cover Art: Clinton Smith
Author Photo: Elizabeth Spencer
Cover Design: Elizabeth Maines McCleavy

Order online: www.finishinglinepress.com
also available on amazon.com

Author inquiries and mail orders:
Finishing Line Press
PO Box 1626
Georgetown, Kentucky 40324
USA

For Robert Spencer

1

I put myself to sleep to look for you again.
I stand on the glass, sky above and below.
Small strands of clouds, no sun yet abundant light.

The cross-legged man said, *you can look.*
I ask where I should start.
Any direction, it extends as far as the dead.

As I walk, I see my reflection in the glass
of a world with no horizon or people,
only silhouettes of breathing machines.

A stoic man, flying like an insect,
straps a mask over my face.
The gray mountains are there: *breathe*, he said.

The clouds draw towards me, vitiated sky—night.
I cry out, *I can't breathe,*
spit up vomit that becomes the sky,

hold a razor to the moles on my side.
Now you know, he said.

2

At 22 I'd pull the plywood off the doors on Hope Street, take two steps,
three steps a time up the termite-eaten stairs past the stripped kitchens
and the stacks of yellow linoleum tiles. I'd dream fill-in the house
with peeps and brohemes, make it an all-nighter crash pad with three
subwoofers, hear The Game through the dark and naked house, that
color of moonlit black that's like a screen turning off.

I took pills from someone in a party bathroom and was followed up the
streets by three black men in Chicago hoodies that were also black. I
can't say they talked to me, if they made sounds with their feet and the
rustling of their clothes.

At Hope and Lehigh there was a baby crawling, no diaper, a mother flinging seeds. I was slurry, looking at this baby crawling through several pieces of flat green broken glass and black plastic from the mirrors of all the Lincolns and some motherfuckin' dude says "it's hot, get down" and I didn't know whether he meant cops or several people behind me but there were five or six pops and then the sounds of a talking baby.

In and out of hospitals in Lancaster I've lost 20 pounds. They biopsied cancer out of a lump on my neck around the time I graduated from the No Drugs Academy. Fuckin' pulling your leg dude, it isn't called that. Shit. The grounds have room for sheep and these alpacas, they look like daughters of giraffes and sheep that had sex.

Dude from Bethlehem got up, talked about hitting his blind grandmother so she'd fall out her wheelchair and spill out tablets that make you shit every hour. He picked 'em up one by one while she was unconscious but he knew she was alive 'cause she snored. After they spring me I go straight to the oncology ward. They'll rip the tumor out and use 4-inch syringes to drain my neck.

Philly doesn't have all 'em tall buildings and that's why I hate New York. No need for bank, I don't have anything other than sweats and a cat I take care of for my folks. They a'ight. Hope and Water Streets, North 5th, could have been Jay-Z until my sources cut me off.

On the corner of Hope, some dude tacked on a top floor that formed more like a crawlspace for hiding people and things than someplace you'd sit. We'd flick lighters up there to get a good draw on the pipe, bats would swoop their black wings in the corners.

They've painted a picture of Obama there now, I'm living to see it, all 'em m-fs thought I wouldn't be, when I was high I did pullups, you grab the edge and go up.

3

The cancer dreams of a tree.
Beehive-like, top parallel to ground,
small branches and brown leaves.

Of a wind that carries small pieces
through the lower levels of the conifers,
squares of bark, flakes, snow.

Of strange disappearances and reappearances,
wind among folded-over dry twigs
on fire, as if in the kiln.

Of storms that carve holes on horizon,
a white stone cut with a scalpel;
not the sailor's visions of red night.

4

What Jasmine tells me:

Martin we are going to have 2 kids together.
One boy, one girl.
You'll show them the things that I cannot show them.
Teach them how to read. You read so well to me.
You are such a snap at making my family comfortable.
Even the stories about buying sweatpants and going to rehab centers.
I thought my family wouldn't love you but they did.

Think of names.
I'll take the lead on teaching the girl how to live, you take the boy.
The boy can play any sport. He'll be strong, know how to use a fork at
a table.
You know you don't use a fork like a shovel, turned sideways.
We won't leave them alone, unloved.
He'll play tennis, excel at math.
You're good, so smart with many things.

5

A lump on my neck the size of a thumb. Crying, like I remembered crying when I was a kid. This was before I knew Jerry, Junk Man, was just someone who dumpster-dived at the QuikChek in Trenton, behind the houses with the hanging lines and Polish and Hungarian girls. Jerry sez I love me some goulash, know it, love some hos who put themselves down and do it on all fours.

I press this lump on my neck and it sends pain down, a centimeter into another level of skin, there are two levels of skin. Pop looks concerned, he always did. Fam never had any money. I was always asking for the debit card and then I took it to the bank and the card would not give me money.

Machine: You do not have sufficient funds. No paper no bars no smack. Jerry would say let's go hit up the mall, turn some shirts, fuck it.

6

The van parked off 322 in Delaware County, looking for its coroner, will be full of stolen Tommy Bahamas.

I've spurred controversy by calling your brother a junky.
The van will be full of things you smoke.

You say, what do you know about my brother.
He tried to sell fake Cartier in North Philadelphia, I said.

Did they carry him off on a flatbed?
Strap him down, measure his pulse.

The van will be full of sweatsocks and muscle drinks,
an old tennis racket.
He always thought he was a badass, I'll say.

Delaware County is dark at night, there are apple orchards,
small hospitals, the industrial ghetto, mothers taking the bus.

7

Coach says: Your tennis and your academics aren't right. Why don't
you take some time.
Think about what you want to do with your life.
I say, it ain't gonna be pro tennis?

Coach:
   I mean, no. Your parents were raising you that way starting from
   young.
   None of you know how tough that is; something special has to be
   there.

   Pros get up every day, work from 6 AM until early afternoon.
   Next day, they condition themselves. Maybe a shorter practice
   routine.
   Every day, they try something specific. Hit hundreds of forehands
   and study how the forehands
   hit the wall, certain rebound angles given a certain velocity. They
   watch their posture so their legs
   don't go. You know your dad has bad knees, right? You watch him
   walk.

   The serves, they're looking at the velocity and spin, getting them
   close to the end-line, through the corners.

8

I'm cold from thinking of you in your cold Pontiac in the burbs
behind the shitty mall where they closed the Limited.
Everything else happened after Dad brought you home.

At Duke University there was a student who lived in his van
to avoid taking out loans for student housing.

If there is a God he will keep you warm.
All these conditional statements.
I learned the idea of the conditional statement teaching literature.

The Duke kid saved $8K or $10K or something, found a way
to cook on a battery-operated heater that made soup tepid,
dried his nose out until it bled. He lived on his "Thai van food,"
often just eating pineapple slices and peanuts for dinner.

My husband could fall asleep at the wheel, turn himself around a
lamppost.

Winter occasionally got bad in North Carolina so the "kid",
rather than breaking down and giving up, wore 4 coats.

I think of you now. After your married girlfriend tossed you
to go back to her old man you barricaded yourself in your G6
and smoked pot for weeks, cracking the window to ventilate
the dope-air out to the playground.

You called our parents, they wouldn't bring you home.
Dad might have forgotten about you late at night but mom never did.

Maybe you scrounged enough to get coffees from WaWa.
I write to you, hope you'll open the cards and envelopes.
I think you won't, don't want you to.

9

With Pop in West Virginia late in August; the men are going down to
the bottom with fishing gear. Putting the twisting worms on the end
of the hooks and throwing back all the shit into the rush of the river,
letting 'em live. Rest of my fam, my older sis, my mom back home
going somewhere.

I ask: Dad, where was mom going to go?

There was a job she had, he begins, voice trailing off, some sort of
hedge fund owned by some men overseas, they were not the nicest
people. She's staying there all night at least I can smoke here. Then
he'd smoke but when I was little he would say don't smoke and if said
I want to smoke he'd reach his white pale hand out and give me a little

tap on the head. Stay alive, Martin. Don't smoke.

I'd always walk behind as he walked down the path past the trailers
down to where the water sparkled and his friend, Burrows, he'd say
you can come here anytime Martin. In West Virginia we were family.

10

I get up, go to buffet, it's eggs, eggs benny with bacon,
old waffles cut into quarters, Notre Dame ad on television.
Nicole says, *Martin appreciates everyone's prayers.*

Marilyn asks when Martin's breath test was, my daughter is
coughing then um-humming, Tommy laughs at her and
kicks OJ into the legs of the hipster server who regards us,
Jehovah's caravan.

There's orange puddles, the distinct odor of infant diarrhea
from someone's dairy intolerance. I didn't say this but
my daughter is milk-bad too.
Nicole says, *take Isabel to the bathroom.*

I rest her flat on the floor. Martin told us yesterday
after radiography revealed that a tumor ate his lung:
I want to fight for life.

I tell my daughter, *don't learn the word depression.*
When I was nearing college, depression led me to PCP.
A flushing toilet and a snorting man interrupt me.

It made me heroic, I continue, *putting bricks*
through the windows of Ford Explorers,
running off with jewelry and Midori bottles.

I stop, redirect: *Isabel, remember that your daddy's a good man.*
Away from the gathering, the bar comforts us.
TVs, NFL talk, young single guys, will those guys

be like me, unable to sit still when the rain hits the windows
on Sunday morning and it's time for church.
I say, *it took me 40 years Isabel*, but she is asleep.

11

When Martin texts me he's funny. He writes Sábado Noche Viva!
and Viva The Hair Formerly Known As Me. In the overnight,
he wanted to have sex with the nurse and even told her.

Martin's heart is Philadelphia's creative vernacular,
its yous and wankster and gangbanger and it ain't my jawn.

My heart grows bright with the belief that Jesus plays
a role in our lives. I sing at the Old Union Methodist choir, comforted
by This Little Light of Mine

Someone stopped me, said "you have been unwell for forty years."
They meant the depression, the way I obsess over bookshelves,

alphabetizing the eight Dick Francis novels I own, deciding it might
be better to place them chronologically, pulling out then reinserting

the stem of my dirty pipe, my teeth an inconsistent amber,
light-brown and dark-brown colorations.

While I was rearranging everything around me, which can only be
a type of rearrangement of myself, I could have been providing some
sort

of example instead of carefully hiding—the way I cruised when
I was a kid and hopeful, not just a seventy-year old man with snowman
hair

who had sex with his wife and ended up needing to protect myself,
with a kid I did not want.

Martin's heart is light for someone who has been in and out
of rehabilitation four times, who had to live outdoors.

In California, he was a drunk on the Santa Barbara beach.
Skater rats alerted the local police to his presence.
Cops combed the edge

of the sand in golf-cart-like things, patrolling for hippies.
I have never been a sleeping man, barely four or five hours

a night, yet when up I'm consumed with the kinds of stupor I associate
with sleep—forgetting everyone's name, mistaking sidewalks for beds,
squirrels for cats.

The last time I talked to my father, I thought he was sleeping on the
floor by the couch, frowning on one side. They inserted plastic straws

into his mouth and fed him through a machine that emitted a giant
sucking noise, vacuumed the stray pieces of food
from between his teeth. He lived 3 more months.

Martin had his chance in one of the therapy sessions
to say what he wanted to say to his mother and me
without fear of reprisal. I tried to say something before it started

but the therapist held a palm up: just let him tell his story.
His story does not have to be your story, his version of events
does not have to be your version, it's nothing you should

feel is the last word on the subject. It's just his turn. When I was a child,
I never spoke out of turn.
I thought, he always spoke out of turn, using words he didn't learn

in our house. Or he dressed in a way appropriated from hip hop.
Meek Mill. Freddie Gibbs. My wife bowed her head slightly as he said
I wondered why my father was home

so often when I was a kid. Other kids' dads they be out somewhere
doing shit, and mine was home in the back of the house,
letting the television run on and on

watching Pete Sampras but not turning on the air conditioner,
I was all fucking hot and stuff, had to go outside 'cause it was cooler than
it was in our house. Nicole would be in another room

taking the nightgown on and off one of her six or seven dolls.
They all looked the same, Martin looked like something
that wasn't the same of anything that I grew up with.

In West Virginia when my father promised me hot dogs,
an evening at the cinema that was in the middle of the town
and often women dressed up because it was the only place

people went out in that place held in a cup of mountains and coal,
of trains winding their way through terrain from which everything
was being extracted or falling.

My wife's black-eyed susans are all I've got this evening, she's off
balancing the books for dirty capitalists. They are all dirty, these
people, they are worse than the people

shooting each other in the street over drugs you light up in glass pipes,
which I only know of because Martin used to try new things
with a glass pipe in the basement, I'd get

sweet smells as if a flower were being cooked on a stove
and come down, see the white smoke flood the widest part
of the glass that was shaped like a cock with testicles.

I started with two Jack and cokes, next, two Dewars and cokes because
I was out of Jack, then my wife telling me
in my memory of Wegman's last Sunday morning,

when I was reaching out for a deviled egg and a fistful of grapes
from a salad bar:
You've been depressed your whole life, it's like your ability

to look for things or support others was suspended while you processed
the fact that you wouldn't be able to get out of bed by 10
more than 2 times out of 3, and the world

was just going to go on around you, other men going to their shining
towers of law and advertising, other women joining them,
or men and women staying home with kids,

you stay home but manage somehow not to be home, I'm not sure
how you do it and yet I still always know you are there. That's comforting.

I defend myself: *I work,* I tell her. I've renovated ceilings, cleaned gutters—
She said, *yeah, you do. It's not much.*
You find your way home by late afternoon.

12

My sis tries to get me to go to the puppy adoption place, but
we saw a Dachshund with a breeder out across from this empty field
in Bristol, the mother bites but you love him when his tail wags,
you get on the floor, flip him. I tell sis now yo, got on my back
to play with him, watch me with Isabel I can entertain, at Christmas

I strapped deer antlers to me like some Disney and crawled on my
tummy, so like the blood goes rushing to my head they remind me
don't smoke or say fuck around the baby. I started giving my tumors
some trees, you got it. No pills or fucking just read how Johnny Cash
abandoned his daughter when he was pill freaking so Isabel looks at me,

I say I'm Rudolph I'm going to bring you a bow and a box and I will
before AA, still go yeh, and I'm the first to make her laugh, rolling in the
dirt without my cigs, my jawn, yeh, just don't want to go underneath,
Rudolph knows there's devils down there, triple-six, fuckin' firestorms,
feel dizzy with that shit growing in my brain when I rotate too quick

13

You say, *why the fuck do you think that? Drugs aren't a lifestyle.*

Because you are still alive.

I know I'll have to explain this to Nicole.
She's been spending more time with him.
Standing at the edges of the racetrack with him
in small Maryland towns.
Hearing more of the stories about drugs, spanning states.

He set his comings and goings around drug levels in plasma.
Set his times to be somewhere around times of others
who approached with hands tucked into coat sleeves.
Gave codes and insight into the invisible economy.

He stands in front of me.
Something like the circling of awareness around a void.
Bulky underneath Pittsburgh Pirates T-shirt.
The Pirates were the West Virginia team,

there being no professional sports there.
He's quiet, laughs more than you'd think
from the mist, the state of stupefaction, the eyes
shifting among three different colors as if magical.

*Drugs fuck you. You look at yourself on drugs you've got a fucking dragon
meteorite in the mirror, looking at you. It's got the same hair and face
you got but it's playing to death with you. It's like if you were in drag, a
store mannequin on junk.*

I tell him, finally. I'd identified it early on,
when I first met Nicole. But now I finally say it
even though it isn't as true now.
There's blood vessels being drawn

into malignancies between the indentations
of his brain; that will eventually become

his lifestyle. He won't be able to get high
because he won't be able to walk.

*Xanax, crack, whatever—you were always passed out even when you
talked. Your fingers quiver, you can't even keep your hands still running
them over your head.*

I regret it immediately, he's starting to lose his hair from the chemo.
His first step is to pat the top of his head, say *it shines*.

14

I used to drive around and forget things because of the brain tumors.
Junk Man was in my basement turning blue. Fucking wack, simply
talking about the weather man, nothing too sinister or run them about
it, then he just slumped the body was stiff and at the same time it was
weightless. I'm like fuck. I was all out of oxycontin so I'd taken Xanax
with a whole bottle of syrup and a little whiskey, a swish of Scope, I
dragged his ass out the door and Mom says, Where are the keys and I
say, Fuck where are the keys and I grab the keys. Mom says, You can't
have the keys, you can't just pick the keys up when you're not able to
drive. And I say, What you want me to do, you want Jerry to die, like,
what, some people aren't worth being alive to you, right, and she said,
No, do what you need to do Martin everyone needs to be alive, and
I'm like thank you, yes, everyone needs, always needs to be alive, and
I chucked him barely conscious into the back and his breath all snotty
and rattle rattle, a big raspy fuck he was just telling me how to decide
whether you would rather be an anarchist someone who grew pot in
Colorado and now here we are. Past Trenton, past Lawrenceville. The
Latino day laborers and peeps who wash windows go to Hispanic night
clubs and fuck those same hot salsalitas in the red dresses bought in the
sto' where I used to steal shit from then try to like sell it back get some
pills I could shit on myself for those pills now, there they are, on the
side of the road all these guys who don't look so good, I pull in and the
car is crunched in half screeeeek and I'm like Jerry, stammering fucker,
can't breathe and the bitches look in the side window and someone
comes over and I'm bleeding all out of my nose and I'm like it's my head
it's my head I have tumors they've been shaken and the po-po says a

wigger got cancer down here and don't it look like Disneyland get out the car and as they pull me out my head and my chest and my head hit the mirror and my chest is a banging against the side of the car and I see a totaled car and I see traffic and I see Jerry and I see and he is not alive and I have a slight nosebleed the faces start to spin with a green dizzy spin then a purple spin then a something nearer a black spin.

15

We warmed ourselves in the hospital
underneath the plastic curtains

gone from being lovers in Europe to
lovers of near-death, our ceiling a

multilinear red monitor, horizon the
gray mountain on a morphine dial

The cloudy windows, smudges of fog,
grain sculpted into river-forks

Stars opened their blue and white stigmas,
your brother inhaled, the oxygen unevenly filling him

Something snapped outdoors, a raft among the life support—
trash, honey, recycled food

The nurse at night reset the corners of the room,
stacked plastic aspirin bottles, wet-naps, rubber stops

I dream of a faceless army of young men
a country full of yurts on fire, animals and children inside

Fleeing goats, ballerinas, fascists along the roads—
you were with me there in that plateau of mud.

The severed limbs, reanimated, crawled to the top of a trellis
of stomach-like trenches and sunned their empty veins

"Do you think he'll walk again," I asked, then
you repeat—"think he'll walk again"

The sun highlights the lead color of his legs,
his stirring sleep warning of division, disconnected

in the way that gray mountains are

16

I try a more complex movement from bed. Turning in the ankles.
When I walked, it was with my feet slightly turned in. My fam noticed
that I was slump shouldered. Never looking down they never noticed
that I walked all off. She: now squeeze Jasmine's hand.

Days to myself. Can think about the muscles that squeeze to hold
a hand inside a hand: net of tendons. I have to listen to tele all day.
When out, never watched. Listened. Music. Games. Sis is more wack
than me with me on this breathing machine.

The man of hers: must have known whether he was her husband or
not her husband.

17

I rise to the task, warn my son he is going to lose his hair
while the nurse rotates him so the sweat
around his thighs doesn't open up bed sores.

I say something about how he won't remember things
and realize I told him the same stuff when we used to find
Ziploc bags full of pot, at least a quarter,

in his upper desk drawer at home. I don't think I actually sounded
different, as if somehow I thought having cancer and using drugs
were two facets of

the same morality. No, they were just two facets of the same man.
I started to think of what he might need when he woke up,
if he could start the radiation again.

Toothbrush. Dreams of something other than being close
to the ground. My stepfather was in hospice for one week.
His skin turned completely white.

When I'm near the end, they'll reiterate that I didn't do much,
look at the penis retracted, wonder what woman made children
with such a man.

18

Yesterday I didn't get a migraine from the tumors. I was a tennis player.
They call those things microvessels, or micro*vasculature*. Mom thinks
I shoot junk in my ass. They thought I'd like totally fucked the car and
ran over a newspaper stack or a stroller. Did I actually play back then?
I can't kill anyone. I'm vital. Show me the pictures. Pull those blinds
down. There's an orange sun like the opening of a Corona bottle.

The world is open all night baby. You got me here? There's bars and
cell phones and shit people made up to be happy. I can't get out. These
clear little electric smokes I have ain't shit. I'm hyper. I'm so way out,
I'm so strong that I'm fighting God. Yesterday his hand reached into
me and said, I'm going to pull out your fucking guts. Baby, I said,
yeah, I talked to God like I loved him. Why didn't you do this a long
time ago, I asked him. Why'd you make me take all these inferior
inventions, whippets and pipes and rolling papers, now that I've got
you how could I want those too.

19

I turned to his mom who wasn't my mom but I called her 'mom'

I asked "is he going to move today" as they rotated the blue leg
caressed the fluid-filled ankle and pressed my thumb into the area
behind the ankle bone

His mom would put down Us Magazine and say he hasn't moved today
and he didn't move yesterday either, but I think he might, I think
they're going to try to rouse him for a bit so you can say hello

We had nothing but time and the gray winter that was like
a big gray horse that breathed at the window where he inhaled

The sound of his snot passed through his lungs as if
he were made of pebbles and rocks, sounded so hard to breathe
and I wondered what it meant when vomit went down your windpipe

Couldn't they make a body that would just push it back up
when you got vomit in your windpipe, or go in and attack

hard things when they were supposed to be soft tissue, just
push the blood out of them like the enemies they were

I thought of all my enemies in this love, cancer and drugs and cars
that could have run through a whole town of five-year-olds, so asleep
he probably was on his drugs

He nods his head for a minute, it covers an inch of space and I feel
blessed by God that at least his neck does not hurt

20

Christmas with the fam, they take sedation down so I can wave.
Fuck-pain like some big sucking Godzilla motherbitch freak pulling
at whatever is left of the meat they've sawed away so they can strap
you to the hospital bed with your own fat and gristle. Then they take

it out and it's like someone slowly is pulling a set of prongs out of the inside of my lungs while some other guy operates a vacuum, they plunge it down the center of my throat, in some unknown ventricle that's between my windpipe and my foodpipe, and crank it. Then just when it hurts most someone starts telling my Mom and Jasmine they have to leave, we have to change him. I can't feel them pawing my ass while they change me. Fuck me.

There's a Christmas tree downstairs, I heard Nicole's squeeze talking about it like I wasn't even here. As if, like, he'd been invited to a room where my disappearing presence wa'n't such a motherfucka. I'm here man. I start to scream, and the vacuum gets worse, pulling the metal prongs off of the lung insides. I'm here. Fucking-A.

When they took me in, I keep on thinking they did my neck civil war style. Like the message on my iPhone, the thing I say to peeps: be your own war. In Spanish: "Sus guerras". Your wars. My wars. The doctor's wars against me. Sharp instruments. No one dreams during sedation. You wake up and see your parts ripped so they can tie you down, make you depend on machines.

I worked. Seven-Eleven, a small telemarketer at night, old person clientele, chimneys and house renos. I got my tats then. I made all look like the combination of Jesus and the devil that I am. I took control of my body.

21

There is a time and space for gray
filling a space the size of an infinite line
in the end the breath has a crackle
in the gray mountains passing through

> somewhere there are no pagodas
> no buddhas and no man-gods
> something imagined
> in the mist of dials switches

in the machine twilight
in the sirens of these
a time and a space for gray
for the enclosure

                                  for walls
                                  of night
                                  in abundance
                                  adumbrating the
walls
there is a
time
the breath

                                  no buddhas no woman-gods
                                  in twilight
                                  something imagined
                                  among the roads

22

On the day you died in another city, I was away
from you, from Nicole, in Raleigh for business,

running after work on a street with three churches,
Christmas trees still glowing with nocturnal crosses,

drawing me past the subject of the Sunday lecture:
does God have a soul? Mentally I rearrange it

to "does God have soul", feel the rebuke of the Cross.
At dinner, I'd thought I'd seen Ivy, whose little boy

died in New York of a rare blood disorder.
On the day of the memorial, the plaza at Lincoln Center

was full of distraught saints, evangelicals.
She pinched her eyes closed with her hands—it looked

like her fingers were crying. I saw Ivy's stand-in,
swirling soda around cracked ice cubes, little child at her side:

no, she would have an adult son by now. On St. Albans,
the runners with searchlights on their heads wave at me

during their night job, part of Meetup Groups, training
for a 5K. I shuffle on, I must go on though every organ

you have is like a hollow orange, full of something murderous.
The lights of the runners fill my eyes,

I see hundreds of them running away from me.

23

we had three months, we tried new favorite restaurants,
in the end chose Bertucci's where he hung out with his father
in high school
we tried out ice skating rinks and ice cream parlors
Peddlar's Market and places where the main focus was bowling
not drugs and beer, not smoking in the parking lot

he'd slept on Venice Beach and saw Hollywood lights
held up department stores and slugged people
just as poor as he was, lacking in spirit or momentum or
"that like fuckin' need to excel", then he said
he was ashamed of all that so he felt the need to give
advice to everyone in WaWa who was making hoagies
putting them on trays talking about getting high
in the same parking lots where he used to get high

one day, I thought he was using again

we were looking into the soulful eyes of my Irish Setter
and he said, I'd never use if you were on my side
then he left for a couple of hours, he said
he had to help his father with something

I had sex with him on the second day and we continued having sex,
today I think I'm having sex with him when I hear the rain
hit the windows of this large house we never would have been able
to afford, I live at home and think he's going to walk through the door
with some shirt that says Mad Lazy, Mad Talented and I'd always say

you're so talented, don't say less about yourself, and he'd say,
I'm talented but man I don't like to get out of bed,
like my other people you know we don't always get up and shit,
and I'd stop him and my father would yell down the stairs
like a man who wanted me to marry a lawyer

24

Nicole and I took a MegaBus to Canal Street and Lafayette,
to a screen print shop next to a Chinatown dive

that had whole ducks cooked for Korean barbecue
rotating in the yellow oven behind the window.

It would be about 500 shirts, a picture of Martin and Jasmine
screenprinted, back from Disneyland.
I'd hoped he would have a year, you said.

Hope is not…I know, you said. Show him the picture.
In the store, Chinese New Year's dragons hung from

tenterhooks, plastic Buddhas set in a small pond with a floor
of smooth white stones, a karaoke version of Silent Night

from a speaker above a stuffed frog and a billboard of selfies.
The shirts, at $1.60 a piece, were $800. I passed different

credit cards across the counter but the machine declined them.
Cash, the guy asked. Don't have it. We could have tried

a smaller quantity, but that seemed uneven, what if someone
who knew the family couldn't get their keepsake when he did die,

we could save up. Why don't we ever have money, you ask me.
The street was unsettling, crowded; a dying man could have hidden

in the throng of pedestrians and people trying on watches,
planning the last act.

That night I remembered a Brooklyn of empty lots,
abandoned animals and rotting fences.

At the edge of a train track covered with Mexican Coca-Cola bottles,
the bus stopped. I reached into my pocket, no fare.

No worries, step on, the driver says. Doesn't look like a driver
so much as a milk delivery man during the Depression.

The bus circles a limited square of parks, bars, brownstones
in front of which a man sells red sneakers.

Advertisements on the bus wall: Safe Sex? Does Debt Keep You
Sleepless. 1-800-SPLIT-UP. To-from on bus interior:

East Williamsburg Industrial Park. I ask the driver
to take me back to Philadelphia to watch Martin die.

We're just circling, he says. When the time comes
to grieve or work, we'll stop. I remember that somehow

I got on without that token. In the spaces between the wooden slats
on the train tracks, daffodils grow in clusters of five or six.

25

I live in your space, windowless save for a 2 by 2 pane, I can
slide it open and feel the wind outside, but this part
of the house does not face the sun

I take the Nautica blue and spray it onto my face, wonder what scents,
clothes of other people were masked by the seduction of this same
bottle, your finger pressing this cologne out in the darkness

at 1:30 AM with the howling of the Prozac cat
keeping me up all night, I turn the lights on and begin to read—

refugees of the Gaza Strip, refugees of the Thai/Cambodian border
after emptying of Phnom Penh, remember decades ago

at 17 and 18 drinking after my parents went to sleep,
holding the 20-pound text about American History,

paragraph about the slaves, a drawing of a scaffold
where they hung "Negros" for unlawful theft of

tools, brandishing weapons, being taught to read.
This was tucked into love songs to America.

I'll listen to the ungrounded socket buzz, blue light of the computer
that's perpetually on, somehow becoming more fundamental
in my concerns since I have stopped eating except
in strict narrow intervals, 6 to 7, 9 to 10, the morning
passes with my hunger

The Gazans stretch sheets over the 80 tons of raw sewage,
planting sticks in the ground to hold them up,

securing the sheet with knots. The Cambodians on the Thai
border fear Pol Pot's agents coming to the non-doorway

doorways of their dwellings, 2 to hold young women down,
one to pull out guns, sharp-ended sticks about an inch in

diameter, plunging themselves, then the sticks into
the women's vaginas, then setting the camp on fire.

The gas from the Gazan sewage could ignite
if the flow was confined to an airtight room.

When the leaking toilet pipe in the basement was too much,
my in-laws just paid a plumber to fix the broken seal.

"Ants ate it away," my father-in-law said. "I've seen that before, but
it's not that common, ants in the sewer pipe sealant."

I've experienced the violence I've brought to myself and those
who love me, the long taunts of my family
over my anger, unable to stop talking to myself, a victim
whose torturer finds previously unexpressed wounds

Your death drew us here to your open room.

Once we realized we would be confined to the darkness
and the sound of the sewage coming from the pipe,

the cats howled, shit on couches, Nicole and I listened together to
the effect of the stress of death on my in-laws, mostly in silences,

strange cell phone usage—late night texts, rolling child toys
tossed about by the family dog, the heavy steps above our heads.

I hear you deep in my dreams where December turns into icy light,
you having overdosed to avoid being awake as cancer killed you,

resettling like dirt and roots closer to the tunnels where
fighters crawl over other fighters to blow the world into fragments.

26

Isabel is a year old and does it now, pulling her sock off
from the space where her big toe should have been.

She exercises her facial muscles and groans like I do
when I'm twisting off the top of a lotion bottle,
waiting for my husband to squeeze off the top.

I start to see in her, as she pulls on the baby gates at
the foot of the stairs, something of all of us.
What did she get from him? This tendency to take her sock off.

What are socks anyway, I ask.
They itch the bottoms of your feet, they discourage or encourage play.
They lead to you sliding on the floor.

Her uncle would have used them I think as puppets.
As my husband does, passionate about driving home to
make socks talk about how it's better to be a Marxist.

And yet, they both needed to have one sock on.
I look at the temperature we keep the house at, a potential explanation.

Her uncle was very entertaining
because he didn't know who Marx was.

27

It was Pop's dream to be president then practice law but he was too
fucking sad.
I told it to the headshrinker. He said: Martin it might make more sense
to you if you tried to focus more on you, being not so sad yourself.

I mean, I know. Yes, you know. He knows. What do you know?
He gets to live, long after I die, he'll get to live, and they'll get to think
about what it was like to watch me focus on being sad. I stop.
Sun's all down outside.

Me and the headshrinker are here together in this small room,
and finally he starts writing all this shit down, I feel it.
Time almost gone.

28

with the faux-fur Russian cap,
photograph of your sister pulling your hair
police and firefighters coming and going with the town siren
tennis racket that knocked off Delaware Valley's #1
filial thick curls of autumn-colored hair

you looked like Vitas Gerulaitis who died from carbon monoxide
poisoning
yet with arms no one could close both hands around
Pastor Mark says, I get choked up, you watched his kids
now we all drink in separate rooms, explore book and television
options
in separate rooms, brought together by

the macho man who chased the Macy's thief across the lot,
you seemed addicted, the no-pain man, got arrested in Macy's
got hoodwinked by a confidence artist in front of the Warhol Museum
left with a baggie that was half dope half catnip
took your brain tumor with you on your trip to Florida
during a near-hurricane

your father says *I called him Martin he called me*—and stops
your grandmother knits you sweaters with purple crosses, you'll never
see the crosses in the reception hall, synced iPod playing Drake
your wife-to-be goes to a hotel room that looks like you,
drinks herself to sleep, old-fashioned grief from trailers to mansions

when my wife and I have no uncle for Isabel
we'll wait for you to smoke Marlboros on the lawn,
we'll wait for you among our other commitments
when the grass smells like Pontiacs of the Grateful Dead
we will ask if you are the ghost, wait out the silence

I waited for about a year
The next man had a political slant, he was from Cyprus

I tried to read magazines with him that had reality show stars
and Fashion Police, articles about Donna Karan's retirement

He'd always put his finger over his lips and say something about
how Ed Snowden better come back to America

I have just returned from babysitting for Nicole
I ask him *who is Ed Snowden*, he calls him
the spiller of state secrets, the world needs him

says Snowden better get back before the Republicans
power through, annihilate the generation of people
who want to fight the man

I told him that was stupid, are they different,
either party, they do the same things
There's still problems with the roads around our house

He looks at me like I'm a dumb walrus or rhino,
as if one of these potholes should just swallow me
after I am done babysitting because the world

needs women to watch kids while men have visions and experiences,
shoot bombs at buildings or other idiots

I dumped him then a few months later heard
some of the same phrases he used on a Kendrick Lamar record

I thought he must have had as much in common with Martin
as I'd originally thought, or had I thought, or had I not

Then I start thinking we could bring Martin back with a séance,
call someone from one of those Polish psychic houses in Cape May
I wouldn't have to talk to anyone else for a couple of days

30

When I gave birth, the way God made my body
knocked me out, but I remember pushing

for hours, the midwife telling me "he's almost here".
I recalled, occasionally, throughout your life
that "almost" meant several hours.

As my second, I thought it would be easier but it wasn't.
Now I tell myself things about your favorite toys,

or, "you always liked adult music, not children's songs";
I go looking for clues about what you were like

when you were two or three in your last self.
I ready for sleep now, brushing my teeth,

pulling the pillows and your childhood stuffed animals
we called Bear and Fox close to me, up to my stomach.

Clinton Smith started writing poetry and playing classical guitar at the age of 12, and has persisted in his interest in writing and music to the present day. His poetry has appeared, most recently, in *Confrontation, Razor Lit,* and *Talking River Review*; he is also currently working on several different stories and a short novel. Born in Vienna, Virginia, outside of DC, he currently lives in Rutledge, Pennsylvania with his family and a pair of cats.

www.ingramcontent.com/pod-product-compliance
Lightning Source LLC
Chambersburg PA
CBHW022100080426
42734CB00009B/1424